Crochet Market Bag Patterns

How to Crochet a Market Bag

Copyright © 2023

All rights reserved.

DEDICATION

Contents

Gathering Rosebuds Market Bag

Supplies:

Caron Cotton Cakes Country Romance #4 Medium Weight 7.5 oz / 460 yds

Size H/8 (5.0 mm) crochet hook

Scissors

Tapestry Needle

Stitch Markers

Approximate finished size: 11" tall from base (not counting strap) x 11" wide base. Strap measures approx 33" long.

Gauge: 8 dc rows x 14 dc st = 4" x 4"

Abbreviations:

MC = magic circle

ch = chain

yo = yarn over

sp = space

dc = double crochet

sl st = slip stitch

st = stitch

sk = skip

blo = back loop only

FPP = front post puff stitch

dc2tog = double crochet 2 st together

sc2tog = single crochet 2 st together

RS = right side

sc = single crochet

Notes about pattern:

ch 3 counts as st at beginning of each round

Optional: for all Flower Puff Stitch rounds, use the end strand of the cake in order to make sure the puffs were a different color from the dc group rounds. You could also work another cake instead.

If you are using 3 colors of yarn for bag: (notes provided throughout pattern for when to change to each color)

Color A: Main color of bag

Color B: Color of flower stem

Color C: Color of flower puff

Special stitches:

dc group = 3 dc st worked in same st

Long dc: dc st worked below into st of previous row indicated.

FPP (front post puff stitch): *yo, insert hook around middle dc of dc group, yo, pull up a loop,* repeat between * * 3 times (9 loops on hook), yo, pull through 8 loops, yo, pull through remaining 2 loops. Note: when working the FPP, be sure to pull up the loops loosely in order to avoid a small, tight stitch.

Instructions:

Bag Base

Crochet Market Bag Patterns

Start with Color A if making bag with 3 different colors of yarn.

Round 1: Make a MC, ch 3 (counts as 1st st), work 11 dc st into MC, sl st top of ch 3. (12)

Round 2: ch 3, dc in same st, 2 dc in each st around, sl st top of ch 3. (24)

Round 3: ch 3, dc in same st, *dc in next st, 2 dc in next st* repeat between * * to last st, dc in last st, sl st to top of ch 3. (36)

Round 4: ch 3, dc in same st, *dc in next 2 st, 2 dc in next st* repeat between * * to last 2 st, dc in last 2 st, sl st to top of ch 3. (48)

Round 5: ch 3, dc in same st, *dc in next 3 st, 2 dc in next st* repeat between * * to last 3 st, dc in last 3 st, sl st to top of ch 3. (60)

Round 6: ch 3, dc in same st, *dc in next 4 st, 2 dc in next st* repeat between * * to last 4 st, dc in last 4 st, sl st to top of ch 3. (72)

Round 7: ch 3, dc in same st, *dc in next 5 st, 2 dc in next st* repeat between * * to last 5 st, dc in last 5 st, sl st to top of ch 3. (84)

Round 8: ch 3, dc in same st, *dc in next 6 st, 2 dc in next st* repeat between * * to last 6 st, dc in last 6 st, sl st to top of ch 3. (96)

Round 9: ch 3, dc in same st, *dc in next 7 st, 2 dc in next st* repeat between * * to last 7 st, dc in last 7 st, sl st to top of ch 3. (108)

Round 10: ch 3, dc in same st, *dc in next 8 st, 2 dc in next st* repeat between * * to last 8 st, dc in last 8 st, sl st to top of ch 3. (120)

Side of Bag

Round 11: ch 3, working in blo, dc in each st around, sl st to top of ch 3. (120)

Round 12: ch 3, working in both loops, 1 dc in each st around, sl st to top of 1st st. (120)

Round 13: repeat round 12. (120)

Note: if you are making bag with 3 different colors of yarn, change to color B.

Round 14: ch 3, 2 dc in same st, sk next 2 st, *3 dc group in next st, sk next 2 st,* repeat between * * around, sl st to 1st st. (120)

For all Flower Puff Stitch rounds, use the end strand of the cake in order to make sure the puffs were a different color from the dc group rounds. You could also use a strand from another cake instead.

Note: If you are making bag with 3 different colors of yarn, change to color C.

Round 15: With 2nd strand of yarn, ch 1, FPP over middle dc of dc group from previous round, *ch 3, FPP over middle dc of next dc group,* repeat between * * to end, ch 3, sl st to 1st st. (40 FPP)

Note: If you are making bag with 3 different colors of yarn, change to color A.

Round 16: With 1st strand of yarn, ch 2, 3 long dc over ch 3 from previous round & between dc group from two rounds below, 3 long dc between each dc group to end, do not sl st join at end of round. (120)

Rounds 17 – 18: 1 dc in each st around. (120)

Note: If you are making bag with 3 different colors of yarn, change to color B.

Round 19: sk next 2 st, *3 dc group in next st, sk next 2 st,* repeat between * * around, do not sl st join. (120)

Note: If you are making bag with 3 different colors of yarn, change to color C.

Round 20: With 2nd strand of yarn, ch 3, FPP over middle dc of dc group from previous round, *ch 3, FPP over middle dc of next dc group,* repeat between * * to end, ch 3, sl st to 1st st. (40 FPP)

Note: if you are making bag with 3 different colors of yarn, change to color A.

Round 21: With 1st strand of yarn, ch 2, 3 long dc over ch 3 from previous round & between dc group from two rounds below, 3 long dc between each dc group to end, do not sl st join at end of round. (120)

Round 22: 1 dc in each st around. (120)

Round 23: *1 dc in next 3 st, dc2tog over next 2 st,* repeat between * * around to end. (96)

Round 24 – 26: repeat rounds 19 – 21

Round 27: *1 dc in next 4 st, dc2tog over next 2 st,* repeat between * * around to end. (80)

Round 28 – 34: 1 dc in each st around. (80)

Round 35 – 36: 1 sc in each st around. (80)

Fasten off. Weave in ends.

Crochet Market Bag Patterns

Strap

Row 1: (RS) ch 16, 1 sc in 2nd ch from hook & in each ch to end. Turn (15)

Row 2: ch 1, 1 sc in each ch to end. Turn. (15)

Row 3 – 6: repeat row 2.

Row 7: ch 1, sc2tog over first 2 st, 1 sc in each st to last 2 st, sc2tog over last 2 st. Turn (13)

Row 8 – 13: repeat rows 2 & 7 (st count = 7 at end of row 13).

Row 14 – 100: repeat row 2.

Row 101: ch 1, 2 sc in same st, 1 sc in each st to last st, 2 sc in last st.

Turn. (9)

Row 102 – 107: repeat rows 2 & 101. (st count = 15 at end of row 107).

Row 108 – 113: repeat row 2.

Turn slightly, now working along side of strap, ch 1, work sc evenly along side of strap. Repeat for opposite side of strap. Leave a long end for sewing before fastening off.

Attach strap with stitch markers leaving 23 stitches between straps on both sides of bag

23 stitches

Sew strap to bag by lining up your strap with top edge of the bag with WS of bag and strap facing out, attach with stitch markers leaving 23 stitches between straps. See photo below. Sew strap to bag using the mattress seam stitch. Weave in ends. Turn right side out.

Boho Grocery Bag

Supplies:

Crochet Hook:

Size US I-9 (5.5 mm) Furls crochet hook

Crochet Market Bag Patterns

Notions:

Yarn needle to weave in ends

Scissors

Stitch Markers

Yarn:

Bernat Handicrafter Cotton

4 Medium Weight yarn

in colorways:

White

Gold

Yardage:

• 130 yards (119 m) white yarn

• 190 yards (174 m) gold yarn

Crochet Market Bag Patterns

Abbreviations/Stitches:

- ch – chain

- dc – double crochet

- sc – single crochet

- st(s) – stitch(es)

Gauge:

11.5 sts and 7 rows = 4" (10 cm)

in double crochet stitch

Measurements/Sizes:

Height: 15" (38 cm)

Width: 16.5" wide (42 cm)

Skill Level:

Advanced Beginner

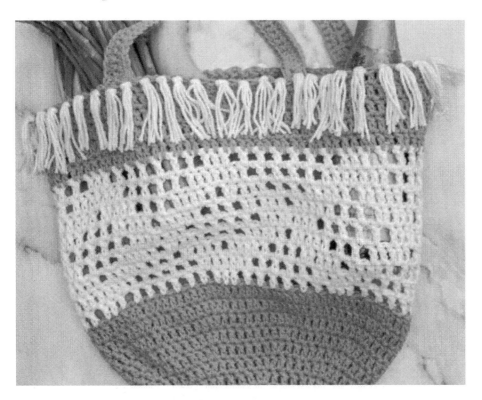

Crochet Boho Grocery Bag Notes:

-This pattern starts with the base of the bag and is worked from bottom up.

-The chain 2 counts as a stitch at the beginning of the round. At the end of each round join to the top of the chain 2.

Crochet Market Bag Patterns

-An alternative to a chain 2 is the Stacked Single Crochet.

Base of Crochet Boho Bag:

Round	Description	Stitch Count
1	Start with Gold Yarn. Inside a Magic Circle dc 8, join.	8
2	Ch 2 (counts as first dc here and throughout), dc in first, 2dc in each remaining stitch around, join. 16	
3	Ch 2, dc in first, dc in next, *2dc in next, dc in next; repeat * around, join.	24
4	Ch 2, dc in first, dc in next 2, *2dc in next, dc in next 2; repeat * around, join.	32
5	Ch 2, dc in first, dc in next 3, *2dc in next, dc in next 3; repeat * around, join.	40
6	Ch 2, dc in first, dc in next 4, *2dc in next, dc in next 4; repeat * around, join.	48
7	Ch 2, dc in first, dc in next 5, *2dc in next, dc in next 5; repeat * around, join.	56

8   Ch 2, dc in first, dc in next 6, *2dc in next, dc in next 6; repeat * around, join.   64

9   Ch 2, dc in first, dc in next 7, *2dc in next, dc in next 7; repeat * around, join.   72

10   Ch 2, dc in first, dc in next 8, *2dc in next, dc in next 8; repeat * around, join.   80

11   Ch 2, dc in first, dc in next 9, *2dc in next, dc in next 9; repeat * around, join.   88

12   Ch 2, dc in first, dc in next 10, *2dc in next, dc in next 10; repeat * around, join.   96

Body of Crochet Boho Bag:

Round	Description	Stitch Count

1   Join White Yarn and Ch 2, (ch 1, skip 1, dc 1) two times, *ch 1, skip 1, dc 3, (ch 1, skip 1, dc 1) six times; repeat * until last 11 stitches, ch 1, skip 1, dc 3, (ch 1, skip 1, dc 1) three times, ch 1 skip 1, join. 96

2   Ch 2, (ch 1, skip 1, dc 1), *ch 1, skip 1, dc 7, (ch 1, skip 1, dc 1) four times; repeat * until last 13 stitches, ch 1, skip 1, dc 7, (ch 1, skip 1, dc 1) two times, ch 1 skip 1, join.   96

3   Ch 2, *(ch 1, skip 1, sc 5) twice, (ch 1, skip 1, dc 1) twice; repeat * until last 16 stitches, (ch 1, sc 5) twice, ch 1, skip 1, dc 1, ch 1, skip 1, join. 96

4   Ch 2, *dc 4, (ch 1, skip 1, dc) twice, ch 1, skip 1, dc 5, ch 1, skip 1, dc 1; repeat * until last 15 stitches, dc 4, (ch 1, skip 1, dc) twice, ch 1, skip 1, dc 5, ch 1, skip 1, join.   96

5   Ch 2, *dc 2, (ch 1, skip 1, dc 1) four times, ch 1, skip 1, dc 5; repeat * until last 15 stitches, dc 2, (ch 1, skip 1, dc 1) four times, ch 1, skip 1, dc 4, join. 96

6   Repeat Round 4 96

7   Repeat Round 3 96

8   Repeat Round 2 96

9   Repeat Round 1 96

Top of Crochet Boho Bag:

Round   Description   Stitch Count

1   Join Gold Yarn, ch 2 (count as first dc), dc in each stitch around, join. 96

21

2-5   Ch 2, dc in each stitch around, join.   96

Fasten off and weave in ends.

Boho Bag Handles (make 2):

Row Description   Stitch Count

1   With Gold Yarn, leaving a long tail for sewing later ch 61, sc in second stitch from hook and across, turn.   60

2-3   Ch 1 (does not count as a stitch), sc across, turn.   60

Fasten off leaving a long tail for sewing to bag. Pin handles on the top of the bag on either side. With yarn needle sew the handles in place. Weave in ends.

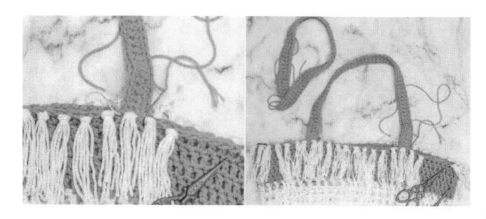

Fringe:

Cut 144 strands of yarn approx. 6 inches in length. Tip: wrapping around an item such as a cell phone and cutting once can speed up the process.

Using 3 strands at a time, tie a larks-head knot on every other stitch at the top of the bag.

To even out the bottom of the fringe lay the bag flat and cut the bottoms of the fringe.

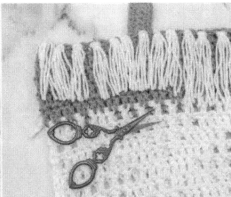

Coffee and Cream Market Bag

Supplies:

Lion Brand Comfy Cotton Blend Mochaccino 4.5 oz / 252 yds (Color A)

Lion Brand Comfy Cotton Blend Whipped Cream 1.75 oz / 98 yds (Color B)

Size J (6.0 mm) crochet hook

Scissors

Tapestry Needle

Stitch Markers

2 Metal D-rings Size 1 1/2"

Approximate finished size: Bag: 16" tall (without handles) x 12" wide
Cords: 24"

Gauge: 6 rows = 4" / 14 dc st = 4"

Abbreviations:

ch = chain

dc = double crochet

dc3tog = double crochet 3 st together (see special stitches section below)

MC = magic circle

Rnd(s) = round(s)

RS = right side

sc = single crochet

sk = skip

sl st = slip stitch

sp = space

st = stitch

yo = yarn over

Notes About Pattern:

ch 3 counts as st at beginning of each round.

Main body of bag is worked in the round. Straps and cords are made separately and sewn to bag at end.

Crochet Market Bag Patterns

Special Stitches:

dc group = 3 dc st worked in same st

dc3tog: *yo, insert hook in next stitch, yo and pull up loop, yo, pull through 2 loops* repeat between * * 2 more times (4 loops on hook), yo, pull through all loops on hook.

Recommended Tutorials:

Granny Triangle Stitch

Romanian Cord Tutorial

Bag Base:

Rnd 1: With Color A, make a MC, ch 3 (counts as 1st st), work 11 dc st into MC, sl st to top of ch 3. (12)

Rnd 2: ch 3, dc in same st, 2 dc in each st around, sl st to top of ch 3.

(24)

Rnd 3: ch 3, dc in same st, *dc in next st, 2 dc in next st* repeat between * * to last st, dc in last st, sl st to top of ch 3. (36)

Rnd 4: ch 3, dc in same st, *dc in next 2 st, 2 dc in next st* repeat between * * to last 2 st, dc in last 2 st, sl st to top of ch 3. (48)

Rnd 5: ch 3, dc in same st, *dc in next 3 st, 2 dc in next st* repeat between * * to last 3 st, dc in last 3 st, sl st to top of ch 3. (60)

Rnd 6: ch 3, dc in same st, *dc in next 4 st, 2 dc in next st* repeat between * * to last 4 st, dc in last 4 st, sl st to top of ch 3. (72)

Rnd 7: ch 3, dc in same st, *dc in next 5 st, 2 dc in next st* repeat between * * to last 5 st, dc in last 5 st, sl st to top of ch 3. (84)

Rnd 8: ch 3, dc in same st, *dc in next 6 st, 2 dc in next st* repeat between * * to last 6 st, dc in last 6 st, sl st to top of ch 3. (96)

Side of Bag:

Rnd 9 – 11: ch 3, 1 dc in each st around, sl st to top of ch 3. (96)

Fasten off Color A

Rnd 12: With Color B, ch 3, 2 dc in same st, sk next 2 st, *3 dc group in next st, sk next 2 st,* repeat between * * around, sl st to top of ch 3.

Rnd 13: ch 2 (counts as 1st st of dc3tog), *yo, insert hook in next stitch, yo and pull up loop, yo, pull through 2 loops* repeat between * * 1 more time (3 loops on hook), yo, pull through all loops on hook, ch 2, **dc3tog, ch 2,** repeat between ** ** to end, sl st to top of ch 3.

Fasten off Color B

Rnd 14: With Color A, sl st into next ch 2 sp, ch 3, 2 dc in same sp, *3 dc group in next ch 2 sp,* repeat between * * to end, sl st to top of ch 3.

Rnd 15: repeat round 13.

Fasten off Color A

Rnds 16 – 25: repeat rounds 14 and 13 changing colors every two rounds.

Rnd 26: With Color A, sl st into next ch 2 sp, ch 3, 2 dc in same sp, *3 dc group in next ch 2 sp,* repeat between * * to end, sl st to top of ch 3.

Rnd 27: With Color A, ch 3, 1 dc in each st around, sl st to top of ch 3. (96)

Rnd 28: repeat round 27.

Rnd 29: ch 1, 1 sc in each st around, sl st to top of ch 3.

Fasten off. Weave in ends.

Straps (make 2):

With Color A, ch 7.

Row 1: 1 sc in 2nd ch from hook and in each ch to end. Turn. (6)

Row 2: ch 1, 1 sc in same st, 1 sc in each st to end. Turn.

Row 3 – 15: repeat row 2.

Fasten off, leaving a long tail for sewing to bag.

Fold 1 strap around each metal D-ring and attach to bag with stitch markers leaving 42 stitches between straps along top edge of bag. With long tail left for sewing, sew to bag using mattress seam stitch method.

Cord (make 3):

Make 3 cords using the Romanian crochet cord method as follows:

With Color A or B (make 2 cords of color A & 1 cord of Color B), ch 2, 1 sc in 2nd ch from hook, 1 sc in loop of skipped ch, turn, 1 sc in 2 loops just under your hook. Continue turning and working 1 sc in 2 loops just under hook after each st made until cord measures approximately 24".

With tails left from each cord, attach cords to metal D-rings on both sides of bag. Weave in end through cord.

Weave in ends.

Tassel (optional):

Make a twisted cord with 1 12" strand of both Colors A & B.

Using a 4" tall book or piece of sturdy cardboard, wrap Color B yarn around height of book approximately 30 – 35 times. Slip yarn off cardboard keeping the circle shape, tie end of twisted cord around the circle of yarn – knot end securely. With A 12" strand of Color A, form a loop on top of the tassel, wrap 1 end of Color A strand around loop and tassel approximately 10 times. Insert end of Color A into loop, pull beginning end of Color A until knot disappears under wrap. Trim ends of strand.

Trim ends of tassel so ends are even. Attach finished tassel to a metal d-ring.

Lattice Market Bag

Supplies:

3 skeins Lily Sugar 'n Cream in Overcast (any worsted weight cotton)

4.5 mm hook

Crochet Market Bag Patterns

yarn needle

scissors

Level

intermediate

Pattern notes & Stitches to Know

magic circle

ch – chain

dc – double crochet

sc – single crochet

· Written in US terms

· ch 3 counts as dc

· ch 1 does not count as sc

· The pattern is made as one entire piece starting at the bottom with joined rounds

LATTICE MARKET BAG CROCHET PATTERN

make a magic circle

Round 1: ch 3, 11 dc in circle, pull circle closed tight, join to first ch 3 with sl st (12 dc)

Round 2: ch 3, dc in same stitch, 2 dc in each stitch around, join to first ch 3 with sl st (24 dc)

Round 3: ch 3, 2 dc in next, *dc, 2 dc in next* repeat from * to * around, join to first ch 3 with sl st (36 dc)

Round 4: ch 3, dc in next, 2 dc in next, *dc in 2 stitches, 2 dc in next* repeat from * to * around, join to first ch 3 with sl st (48 dc)

Round 5: ch 3, dc in next 2, 2 dc in next, *dc in 3 stitches, 2 dc in next* repeat from * to * around, join to first ch 3 with sl st (60 dc)

Round 6: ch 3, dc in next 3, 2 dc in next, *dc in 4 stitches, 2 dc in next* repeat from * to * around, join to first ch 3 with sl st (72 dc)

Round 7: ch 3, dc in next 4, 2 dc in next, *dc in 5 stitches, 2 dc in next* repeat from * to * around, join to first ch 3 with sl st (84 dc)

Round 8: ch 3, dc in next 5, 2 dc in next, *dc in 6 stitches, 2 dc in next* repeat from * to * around, join to first dc with sl st (96 dc)

Round 9: ch 3, dc in next 6, 2 dc in next, *dc in 7 stitches, 2 dc in next* repeat from * to * around, join to first dc with sl st (108 dc)

Round 10: ch 3, 2 dc in same stitch, ch 2, skip 3 stitches, sc in next, ch 5, skip 3 stitches, sc in next, ch 2, *skip 3 stitches, 5 dc in next, ch 2, skip 3 stitches, sc in next, ch 5, skip 3 stitches, sc in next, ch 2* repeat from * to * around, to last 3 stitches, skip 2 stitches, 2 dc in last, join to first ch 3 with sl st

Round 11: ch 4 (counts as dc + ch 1), dc in next, ch 1, dc in next, ch 2, sc in ch 5 space, ch 2, *(dc in next dc, ch 1) four times, dc in next, ch 2, sc in ch 5 space, ch 2* repeat from * to * around, to last 2 stitches, (dc in next dc, ch 1) twice, join to first ch 3 with sl st

Round 12: ch 5 (counts as dc + ch 2), dc in next, ch 2, dc in next, *(dc in next dc, ch 2) four times, dc in next* repeat from * to * around to last 2 dc, (dc in next dc, ch 2) twice, join to first ch 3 with sl st

Round 13: ch 3, 2 dc in ch 2 space, dc in dc, 2 dc in ch 2 space, dc between next 2 dc, *(2 dc in next ch 2 space, dc in dc) three times, 2 dc in next ch 2 space, dc in between next 2 dc* repeat from * to * around, to last 2 dc, 2 dc in ch 2 space, dc in dc, 2 dc in ch 2 space, join to first ch 3 with sl st

Round 14 – 25: repeat rounds 10 – 13 three more times

Round 26 – 27: ch 3, dc in each stitch around, join to first ch 3 with sl st (108 dc)

STRAP

Row 1: ch 1, sc in 8 stitches (8 sc)

Row 2 – 61: ch 1, turn, sc in each stitch across (8 sc)

Fasten off. Leave a long end for sewing.

Sew the last row of the strap to the opposite side of the bag from where the strap started (46 stitches from row 1 of the strap).

Sew with a whip stitch using the long end.

Weave in all the ends.

Caldwell Market Bag

Materials:

US size H/8, 5.0 mm crochet hook

Paintbox Yarns Cotton Aran (category 4, worsted weight yarn)

Crochet Market Bag Patterns

*2.8 oz of contrasting color (Light Champagne – 2 skeins)

*5.9 oz of main color (Melon Sorbet – 4 skeins)

Large Eye Yarn Needle

Approx. 72" of ½" Cotton Rope (optional)

Abbreviations:

ch: chain

puff: puff stitch (see notes)

dc: double crochet

sl st: slip stitch

sp: space

st: stitch

BLO: back loop only

Sc2tog: single crochet 2 together

Finished Size: Approximately 15" wide and 13" tall (measured to the lowest point on the top of the bag- 29" tall including handles). Each square measure 5.5" by 5.5".

Gauge: gauge is not critical

Notes:

The first 4 puff stitches of the pattern have an extra yarn over compared to the rest of the puff stitches.

1st puff stitches: [yo, pull up a loop] 4 times (9 loops on the hooks), yo, pull through all 9 loops on the hook. (Only used for Round 1.)

puff stitch: [yo, pull up a loop] 3 times (7 loops on the hooks), yo, pull through all 7 loops on the hook. (Used for all puff stitches after Round 1.)

After round 2, stitches are either worked in the ch-3 space between 2 puff stitches or in the ch-1 space between 2 double crochets.

Crochet Market Bag Patterns

When working Round 1 of the top border, work 20 single crochets on each side of the square working in each dc, puff, and ch-1 space.

Front & Back of bag: Both sides of the bag are identical, but for ease of working the pattern, especially the top border, pick a side to be the front.

If you joined your squares differently, your stitch counts for the top border may not match mine, which is totally fine. Just work to get those three border rows to lie nice and flat.

Instructions:

Making the Squares:

Make 13 squares total

Start with a magic circle

Round 1: [Puff (see notes), ch 3] 4 times, tighten to close, join with a sl st in the 1st puff.

Round 2: [(Puff, ch 3, puff, ch 1) in ch-3 sp, (dc, ch 1, dc) in puff] 4 times, join with a sl st in the 1st puff.

Round 3: (Puff, ch 3, puff, ch 1, dc, ch 1, dc) in ch-3 sp, (dc, ch 1, dc) in ch-1 sp, [(dc, ch 1, dc, puff, ch 3, puff, ch 1, dc, ch 1, dc) in ch-3 sp, (dc, ch 1, dc) in ch-1 sp] 3 times, (dc, ch 1, dc) in 1st ch-3 sp (the same ch-3 sp you started the round in), join with a sl st in the 1st puff.

Round 4: (Puff, ch 3, puff, dc,) in ch-3 sp, [(dc, ch 1, dc) in ch-1 sp] 3 times, [(dc, puff, ch 3, puff, dc) in ch-3 sp, {(dc, ch 1, dc) in ch-1 sp} 3 times] 3 times, dc in 1st ch-3 sp (the same ch-3 sp you started the round in), join with a sl st in the 1st puff.

Round 5: (Puff, ch 3, puff, dc, ch 1, dc) in ch-3 sp, [(dc, ch 1, dc) in ch-1 sp] 3 times, [(dc, ch 1, dc, puff, ch 3, puff, dc, ch 1, dc) in ch-3 sp, {(dc, ch 1, dc) in ch-1 sp} 3 times] 3 times, (dc, ch 1, dc) in 1st ch-3 sp, join with a sl st in the 1st puff.

Round 6: (Puff, ch 3, puff, dc,) in ch-3 sp, [(dc, ch 1, dc) in ch-1 sp] 5 times, [(dc, puff, ch 3, puff, dc) in ch-3 sp, {(dc, ch 1, dc) in ch-1 sp} 5 times] 3 times, dc in 1st ch-3 sp (the same ch-3 sp you started the round in), join with a sl st in the 1st puff.

Fasten off and weave in ends.

Assembling the bag:

Lay out the squares according to the diagram below and use an invisible seam or other favorite join stitch to sew the squares together.

Once your squares are joined, fold the bag so the bottom two squares line up with the top two squares. Line up the sides of the bag and sew both sides closed according to the color-coded lines in the diagram. Weave in ends.

Adding the top border:

Round 1:

Join yarn in ch-3 sp at the right side of the front of the bag.

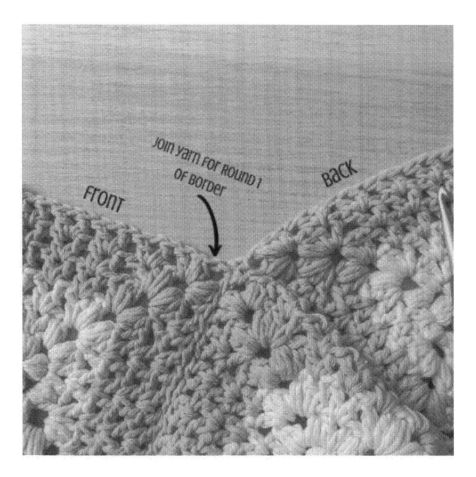

2 sc in ch-3 sp, *sc in the next 20 sts, 5 sc in ch-3 sp, sc in the next 20 sts, [2 sc in ch-3 sp] 3 times, sc in the next 20 sts, 5 sc in ch-3 sp, sc in the next 20 sts*, [2 sc in ch-3 sp] 2 times, repeat from * to *, 2 sc in ch-3 sp, join with a sl st to the 1st sc.

Round 2: work BLO

ch 1, sc in the next 24 sts, 3 sc in next st, sc in the next 24 sts, sc2tog, sc in the next 24 sts, 3 sc in next st, sc in the next 23 sts, sc2tog, sc in the next 23 sts, 3 sc in next st, sc in the next 24 sts, sc2tog, sc in the next 24 sts, 3 sc in next st, sc in the next 23 sts, sk last sc, join with a sl st to the 1st sc.

Round 3: sl st in each st around, join with a sl st. Fasten off and weave in ends.

Adding Handles:

Cut 2 36" lengths of rope. Push the rope, back to front through both top ch-3 spaces on one side of the bag so that the ends of the rope face outward. Tie a knot in each end. Flip the bag over and attach rope to the other side.

Start with a magic circle

Round 1:

[Puff (see notes), ch 3] 4 times, tighten to close, join with a sl st in the 1st puff.

Round 2:

[(Puff, ch 3, puff, ch 1) in ch-3 sp, (dc, ch 1, dc) in puff] 4 times, join with a sl st in the 1st puff.

Round 3:

(Puff, ch 3, puff, ch 1, dc, ch 1, dc) in ch-3 sp,

(dc, ch 1, dc) in ch-1 sp,

[(dc, ch 1, dc, puff, ch 3, puff, ch 1, dc, ch 1, dc) in ch-3 sp, (dc, ch 1, dc) in ch-1 sp] 3 times,

(dc, ch 1, dc) in 1st ch-3 sp, join with a sl st in the 1st puff.

Round 4:

(Puff, ch 3, puff, dc,) in ch-3 sp, [(dc, ch 1, dc) in ch-1 sp] 3 times, [(dc,puff, ch 3, puff,dc) in ch-3 sp, {(dc, ch 1, dc) in ch-1 sp} 3 times] 3 times, dc in 1st ch-3 sp (the same ch-3 sp you started the round in), join with a sl st in the 1st puff.

The "v" on the front of the bag (it is the same on the back) has 3 chain

3 spaces

2 sc in ch-3 sp] 3 times,

Acorn Market Bag

Supplies:

Katia Lino 100% yarn, 1 ball beige, 1 ball yellow and 1 ball green. Ball size is 50g. Crochet hook is 3 mm. My bag measures about 12 inches

Crochet Market Bag Patterns

wide and 12 inches long.

Abbreviations:

R = round

ch = chain

dc = double crochet

sl st = slip stitch

beg = beginning

dc2tog = double crochet 2 together

dc3tog = double crochet 3 together

Bag base – with 1st color make a magic ring.

R1 – ch 3 (counts as 1st dc here and throughout), dc 1 in the ring, ch 2, (dc 2, ch 2) repeat 7 times (total 8 dc2-parts), sl st in beg 3rd ch.

R2 – ch 3, dc 1 in next dc, dc 1 in ch2-space, ch 2, *dc 1 in each next 2 dc, dc 1 in ch2-space, ch 2, repeat from*, sl st in beg 3rd ch.

R3 – ch 3, dc 1 in each next 2 dc, dc 1 in ch2-space, ch 2, *dc 1 in same ch2-space, dc 1 in each next 3 dc, dc 1 in next ch2-space, ch 2, repeat from*, end the round with 1 dc in same ch2-space, sl st in beg 3rd ch.

R4 – ch 3, dc 1 in each next 3 dc, dc 1 in ch2-space, ch 2, *dc 1 in same ch2-space, dc 1 in each next 5 dc, dc 1 in next ch2-space, ch 2, repeat from*, end the round with 1 dc in same ch2-space and 1 dc in next dc, sl st in beg 3rd ch.

R5 – ch 3, dc 1 in each next 4 dc, dc 1 in ch2-space, ch 2, *dc 1 in same ch2-space, dc 1 in each next 7 dc, dc 1 in next ch2-space, ch 2, repeat from*, end the round with 1 dc in same ch2-space and 1 dc in each next 2 dc, sl st in beg 3rd ch.

R6 – ch 3, dc 1 in each next 5 dc, dc 1 in ch2-space, ch 2, *dc 1 in same ch2-space, dc 1 in each next 9 dc, dc 1 in next ch2-space, ch 2, repeat from*, end the round with 1 dc in same ch2-space and 1 dc in each next 3 dc, sl st in beg 3rd ch.

R7 – ch 3, dc 1 in each next 6 dc, dc 1 in ch2-space, ch 2, *dc 1 in same ch2-space, dc 1 in each next 11 dc, dc 1 in next ch2-space, ch 2, repeat from*, end the round with 1 dc in same ch2-space and 1 dc in each next 4 dc, sl st in beg 3rd ch.

R8 – ch 3, dc 1 in each next 7 dc, dc 1 in ch2-space, ch 2, *dc 1 in same ch2-space, dc 1 in each next 13 dc, dc 1 in next ch2-space, ch 2, repeat from*, end the round with 1 dc in same ch2-space and 1 dc in each next 5 dc, sl st in beg 3rd ch.

R9 – ch 3, dc 1 in each next 8 dc, dc 1 in ch2-space, ch 2, *dc 1 in same ch2-space, dc 1 in each next 15 dc, dc 1 in next ch2-space, ch 2, repeat from*, end the round with 1 dc in same ch2-space and 1 dc in each next 6 dc, sl st in beg 3rd ch.

R10 – ch 3, dc 1 in each next 7 dc, dc2tog in next 2 dc, ch 2, in next ch2-space dc2tog, ch 2, *dc2tog in next 2 dc, dc 1 in each next 13 dc, dc2tog, ch 2, in next ch2-space dc2tog, ch 2, repeat from*, end the round with dc2tog and 1 dc in each next 5 dc, sl st in beg 3rd ch.

R11 – ch 3, dc 1 in each next 6 dc, dc2tog in next 2 dc, ch 2, (in next ch2-space dc2tog, ch 2) twice, *dc2tog in next 2 dc, dc 1 in each next 11 dc, dc2tog, ch 2, (in next ch2-space dc2tog, ch 2) twice, repeat from*, end the round with dc2tog and 1 dc in each next 4 dc, sl st in beg 3rd ch.

R12 – ch 3, dc 1 in each next 5 dc, dc2tog in next 2 dc, ch 2, (in next ch2-space dc2tog, ch 2) three times, *dc2tog in next 2 dc, dc 1 in each next 9 dc, dc2tog, ch 2, (in next ch2-space dc2tog, ch 2) three times, repeat from*, end the round with dc2tog and 1 dc in each next 3 dc, sl st in beg 3rd ch.

R13 – ch 3, dc 1 in each next 4 dc, dc2tog in next 2 dc, ch 2, (in next ch2-space dc2tog, ch 2) four times, *dc2tog in next 2 dc, dc 1 in each next 7 dc, dc2tog, ch 2, (in next ch2-space dc2tog, ch 2) four times, repeat from*, end the round with dc2tog and 1 dc in each next 2 dc, sl st in beg 3rd ch.

R14 – ch 3, dc 1 in each next 3 dc, dc2tog in next 2 dc, ch 2, (in next ch2-space dc2tog, ch 2) five times, *dc2tog in next 2 dc, dc 1 in each next 5 dc, dc2tog, ch 2, (in next ch2-space dc2tog, ch 2) five times, repeat from*, end the round with dc2tog and 1 dc in next dc, sl st in beg 3rd ch.

R15 – ch 3, dc 1 in each next 2 dc, dc2tog in next 2 dc, ch 2, (in next ch2-space dc2tog, ch 2) six times, *dc2tog in next 2 dc, dc 1 in each next 3 dc, dc2tog, ch 2, (in next ch2-space dc2tog, ch 2) six times, repeat from*, end the round with dc2tog, sl st in beg 3rd ch.

R16 – sl st in next dc, ch 3, dc2tog in next 2 dc, ch 2, (in next ch2-space dc2tog, ch 2) seven times, *dc2tog in next 2 dc, dc 1 in next dc, dc2tog, ch 2, (in next ch2-space dc2tog, ch 2) seven times, repeat from*, end the round with dc2tog, sl st in beg 3rd ch.

R17 – ch 3, dc 1 in next dc, ch 2, (in next ch2-space dc2tog, ch 2) eight times, *dc3tog in next 3 dc, ch 2, (in next ch2-space dc2tog, ch 2) eight times, repeat from*, end the round with = start dc and leave last 2 loops on hook, insert hook in beg dc (not 3rd ch), yarn over and pull through 2 loops on hook. Fasten off, cut of the 1st color.

Bag body – join the 2nd color in last st of previous round.

R18 – ch 3, dc in next ch2-space, ch 1, *dc2tog = insert hook in next dc, pull up loop, pull through first 2 loops, insert hook in next ch2-space, pull up loop, pull through first 2 loops, yarn over and pull through all 3 loops on hook, ch 1, repeat from*, finish the round with sl st in beg dc (not 3rd ch).

R19 – ch 3, dc in next ch1-space, ch 1, *dc2tog = insert hook in next dc, pull up loop, pull through first 2 loops, insert hook in next ch1-space, pull up loop, pull through first 2 loops, yarn over and pull through all 3 loops on hook, ch 1, repeat from*, finish the round with sl st in beg dc (not 3rd ch).

R20-29 – repeat R19. Each round has 144 st. Fasten off, cut off the 2nd color.

Edge and handles – count 30 st from last st of previous round and join the 3rd color with sc.

Sc total 30 including the 1st sc, turn.

Ch 1, sc 1 in each sc, turn.

Make total of 5 rows, fasten off, cut off yarn.

Count 42 st on last round of 2nd color to skip and join 3rd color with sc in next st.

Sc total 30 including the 1st sc, turn.

Ch 1, sc 1 in each sc, turn.

Make total of 5 rows, don't cut off.

Turn 5 rows sideways, ch 1, sc 1 in each side st of 5 rows, skip next st of 2nd color, sc 1 in each next dc2tog and ch1-space (40 st), skip next st, sc 1 in each side st of 5 rows.

Ch 100 for the first handle, making sure the long chain is not twisting, reach over the 30 sc and sc 1 in each side st of 5 rows. Handle chain will arch over the 5 sc rows.

Crochet Market Bag Patterns

Skip next st of 2nd color, sc 1 in each next dc2tog and ch1-space (40st), skip next st, sc 1 in each side st of 5 rows.

Ch 100 for the second handle, reach over the 30 sc (again the handle chain will arch over the 2nd set of 5 rows) and start continuous round with *sc in each 5 side sc, sc in each next 40 sc, sc in each 5 side sc, sc in each 100 ch, repeat from* on the other side.

Work total of 4 continuous rounds. You will have 4 sc rounds on handles and 5 sc rounds on edge. Fasten off, cut off the 3rd color.